MAZE MANIA

Age-Proof Your Brain!

Puzzle Constructors: Myles Callum, Don Cook, Adrian Fisher, David Helton, Robin Humer, Steve Karp, Planet X Graphics, Pete Sarjeant, Andy Scordellis, Jen Torche, Alex Willmore

Illustrators: Helem An, Robin Humer, Jen Torche

Cover Puzzle: Adrian Fisher

Brain Games is a trademark of Publications International, Ltd.

© **2011 Publications International, Ltd.**

ISBN-13: 978-1-4508-2843-7
ISBN-10: 1-4508-2843-4

Manufactured in USA.

8 7 6 5 4 3 2 1

Mazzle

Don't get too caught up in all the twists and turns as you negotiate your way to the center of this intricate labyrinth.

Answer on page 28.

Over, Under, and Out

Cross over and under bridges to reach the end of this maze.

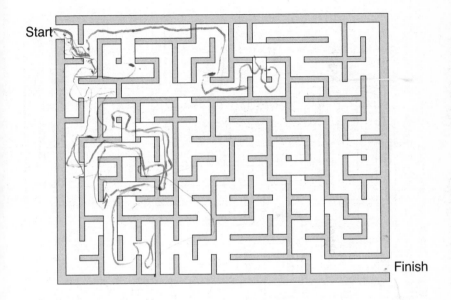

Start

Finish

Answer on page 28.

3

Golf

Line up the putt to get a hole in one as you go through the maze.

Answer on page 28.

4

Astonishing Argyle

Find your way through all the twists and turns of this argyle pattern maze.

Finish

Start

Answer on page 28.

Runaway Train

You're on a runaway train that won't stop moving forward! The path from start to finish must follow the curve of the loops; sharp turns aren't allowed.

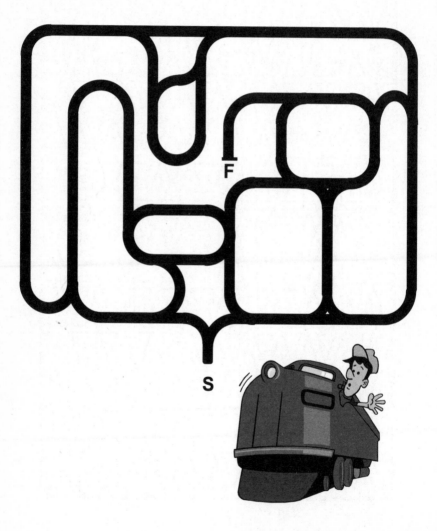

Answer on page 28.

Butterfly

Find your way through the pattern of the butterfly's wing.

Start

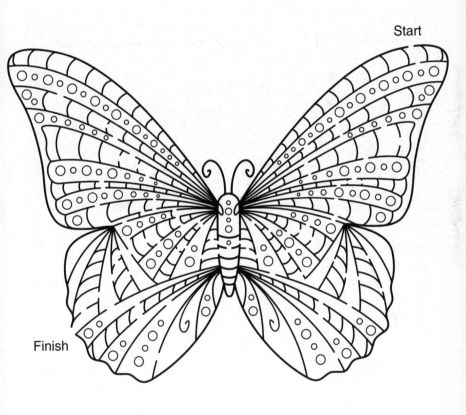

Finish

Answer on page 29.

Get It Straight

Don't get too caught up in all the twists and turns as you negotiate your way to the center of this intricate labyrinth.

Answer on page 29.

Here Kitty!

Uh-oh! Looks like kitty is stuck on the roof of the neighbor's house again. Can you find your way through the haunted rooms to the roof?

Answer on page 29.

Oh, Waiter!

There's a fly in his soup! Go pick up the soup from the disgruntled diner, take it back to the chef's window (at the "top" of the "room"), pick up the new bowl prepared by the chef, and get it back to that hungry patron before it gets cold.

Answer on page 29.

Swing Batter!

Follow the path of the ball from the pitcher to the batter.

Answer on page 29.

Jammed Tractor

Your tractor is jammed and you can only go forward or turn left!

Answer on page 29.

Dig a Hole

Dig your way through the center of the Earth from Australia to Spain.

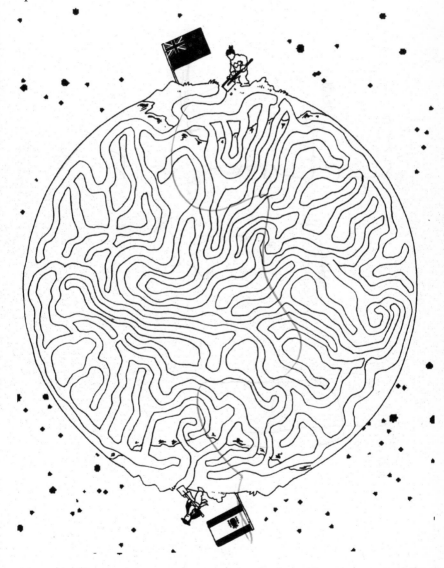

Answer on page 30.

At the Mall

Help Mary find her way to the food court to meet her friend, Cynthia.

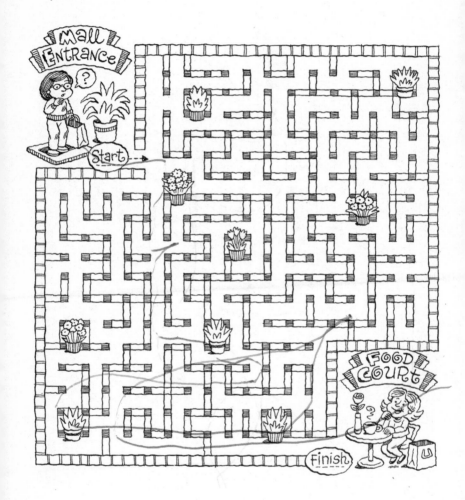

Answer on page 30.

Get It Straight

Don't get too caught up in all the twists and turns as you negotiate your way to the center of this musical labyrinth.

Answer on page 30.

You Are Here

...and the taxi meter is ticking. This professional building is a maze of corridors and cubicles. Elevators are local or express only; there are no stairs. And over-stressed office workers won't give you directions to the exit. Why, oh why, did you ever come in here? Doesn't matter now—time to get moving!

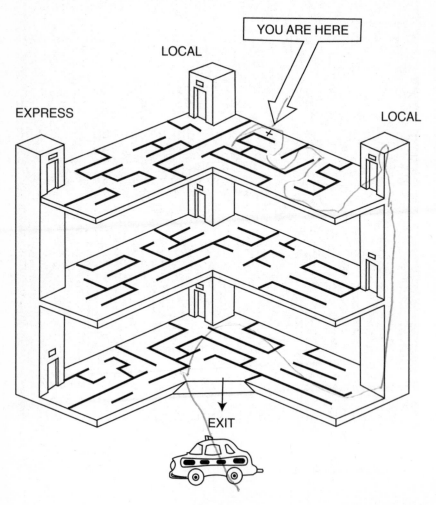

Answer on page 30.

Flower Maze

Work your way to the top through the leaves and petals of this flower maze.

Answer on page 30.

Otter

Help the river otter get dinner by finding a clear path to the crayfish.

Answer on page 30.

Bike Maze

Burt will enjoy a snow cone after his bike ride, but first he must find his way through this twisting bike trail.

Answer on page 31.

An Easel Maze

Guide your paintbrush to the easel to finish your painting and get out of the maze.

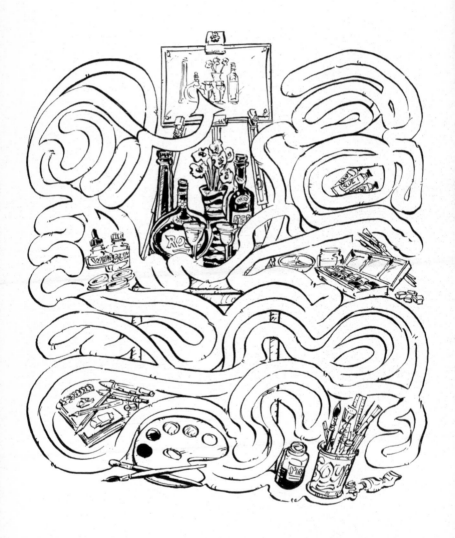

Answer on page 31.

Treasure Castle

The knight must choose the right path from start to finish that will help him avoid the dragon and lead him to riches.

Answer on page 31.

Robot

This poor robot has broken down! Help restore power to him by connecting the circuit from the fuse in his left leg to the battery pack in his chest.

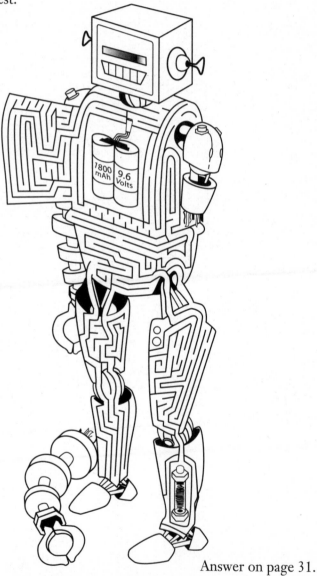

Answer on page 31.

Wrong Number

This mom is trying to order pizza for her kids. Can you guide her call to the pizza parlor? Be careful not to get the wrong number!

Answer on page 32.

Space Race

Help the astronaut land on the moon by navigating the spaceship through the solar system.

Answer on page 32.

Clock

Don't run out of time! Help the mouse find the cheese at the end of the maze. The mouse can travel around loops.

Answer on page 32.

Mazzle

Don't get too caught up in all the twists and turns as you negotiate your way to the center of this intricate labyrinth.

Answer on page 32.

Get It Straight

Don't get too caught up in all the twists and turns as you negotiate your way to the center of this unicorn labyrinth.

Answer on page 32.

ANSWERS

Mazzle (page 2)

Over, Under, and Out (page 3)

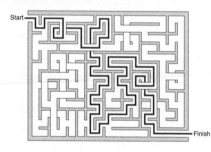

Golf (page 4)

Astonishing Argyle (page 5)

Runaway Train (page 6)

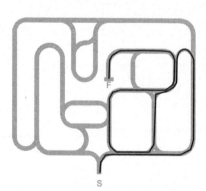

28

Butterfly (page 7)

Oh, Waiter! (page 10)

Get It Straight (page 8)

Swing Batter! (page 11)

Here Kitty! (page 9)

Jammed Tractor (page 12)

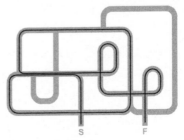

Dig a Hole (page 13)

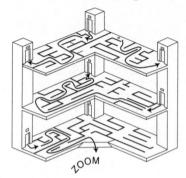

You Are Here (page 16)

At the Mall (page 14)

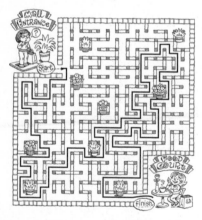

Flower Maze (page 17)

Get It Straight (page 15)

Otter (page 18)

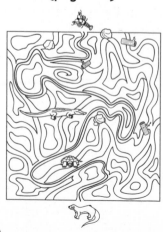

Bike Maze (page 19)

Treasure Castle (page 21)

An Easel Maze (page 20)

Robot (page 22)

Wrong Number (page 23)

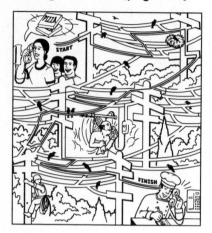

Clock (page 25)

Space Race (page 24)

Mazzle (page 26)

Get It Straight (page 27)

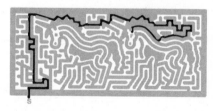